The Picnic

Written by Catherine Baker
Illustrated by Alan Rowe

Collins

lots of picnic food

a dish of corn

lots of picnic food

a dish of corn

a man surfs

red and pink hoops

a man surfs

red and pink hoops

wet fur on the dog

torn red shorts

wet fur on the dog

torn red shorts

 Review: After reading

Use your assessment from hearing the children read to choose any GPCs, words or tricky words that need additional practice.

Read 1: Decoding

- On page 2, point to the word **food**. Ask: Which two letters make the /oo/ sound? (*oo*). Turn to page 9 and ask the children to find and read the word with the same sound. (**hoops**)
- Ask the children to read these words. Can they find the digraphs (the two letters making one sound)?

  corn (*or*)   **fur** (*ur*)   **surfs** (*ur*)   **torn** (*or*)   **shorts** (*sh, or*)

Read 2: Vocabulary

- Look back through the book and discuss the pictures. Encourage children to talk about details that stand out for them. Use a dialogic talk model to expand on their ideas and recast them in full sentences as naturally as possible.
- Work together to expand vocabulary by naming objects in the pictures that children do not know.
- On pages 6 and 7, challenge the children to explain how to surf or how to play with the hoops.

Read 3: Comprehension

- On pages 2 and 3, ask: Which picnic foods would you like most? How do they taste?
- Look together at the scene on pages 14 and 15, and encourage the children to talk about what is happening. What would they like to do if they went on a picnic by the sea?